A se ... aste cartoons
from ... y–Jex Partnership

PRINTED IN ENGLAND BY MERLIN COLOUR PRINTERS, CANVEY ISLAND
ISBN 0 907280 25 0
SILVEY-JEX PUBLICATIONS, 14 CHALDON ROAD, LONDON SW6 7NJ

"I'll get you for this"

"It started as a bird-bath but Geoffrey got carried away."

"Not you – bugger off"

"Do you mind sticking your beak elsewhere"

*"I love crowds...
there's no shit and miss with crowds"*

"Quick – hot water and plenty of it"

"We're too low Skipper...that's a budgie."

"Swanee...how I love ya, how I love ya..."

"OWL!"

"Got myself laid last night."

"There's a lot of tits on the bird table this morning."

"CHRIST! THIS MUST BE OUR LUCKY DAY"

"Fancy giving the 'kiss of life' to a dying budgie you daft bitch."

SUPER
GLUE

"That's it...let them eat off your hand."

"There we are."

"Are you sure you want to go ahead with this stunt."

"God, you're disgusting."

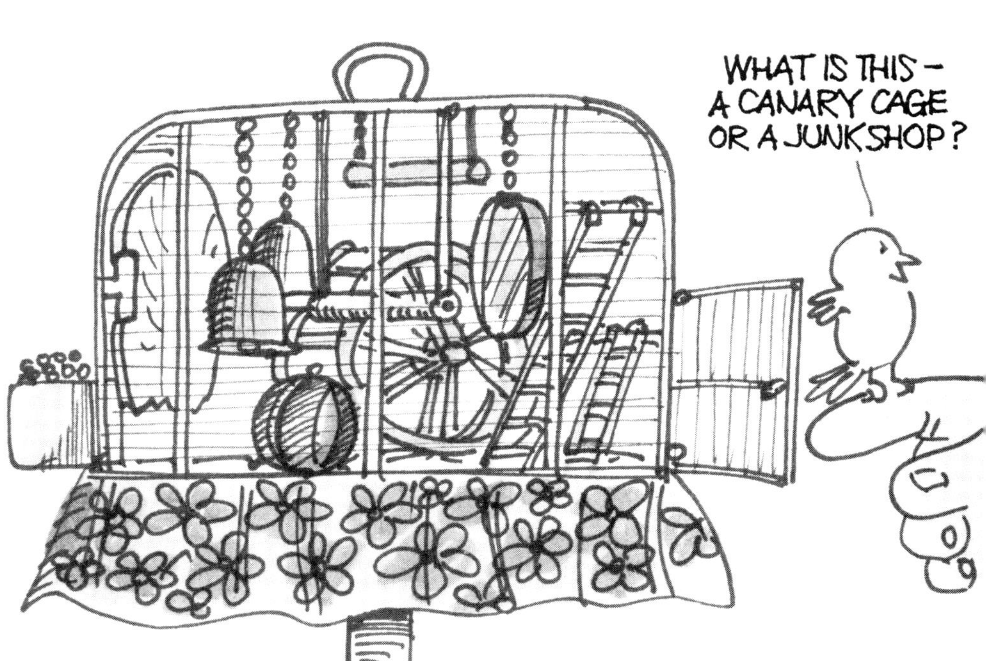
WHAT IS THIS –
A CANARY CAGE
OR A JUNKSHOP?

"It was Doris's idea, to stop him crapping on the carpet."

"Oh...you're early."

"Tell me, do you hang your pheasants?"
"No, shoot 'em usually."

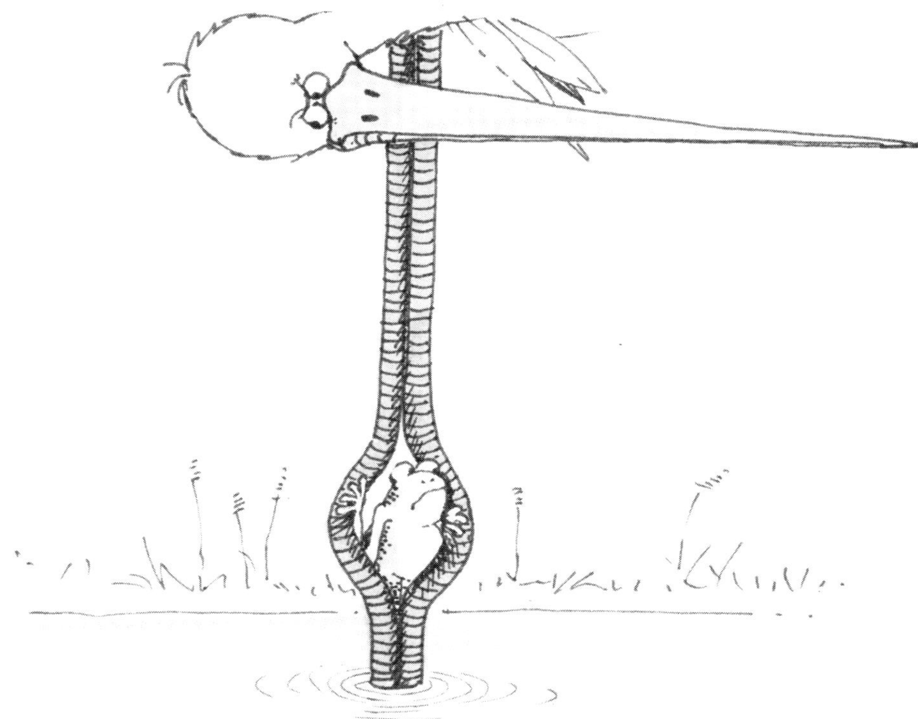

"Christ...did you see that?"